The Widow Oil Tycoon

10 Keys to Turn Your Pot of Oil into an Oil Field

L. Renee Richardson, MBA

The Widow Oil

Tycoon

10 Keys to Turn Your Pot of

Oil into an Oil Field

L. Renee Richardson, MBA

L. Renee Richardson, MBA

ISBN-13: 978-0-578-49370-1

Unless otherwise indicated, all Scripture quotations are taken from

the King James Version (KJV) of the Holy Bible.

Library of Congress Cataloging-in Publication

Data has been applied for.

Printed in the United States of America

DEDICATION

This book is dedicated to my loving husband, Glen, and my wonderful parents SGM (retired) and Dr. Laverne M. Taylor. My husband always tells people if they were looking for the top ten people to run the world, L. Renee would be one of them. His long-term vision to leave an inheritance to our grandchildren led us on the new journey of entrepreneurship and the launch of RTM8, our family conglomerate. My parents are living examples of how to build Wealth and Riches™. They have instilled in us a wisdom and knowledge that is powerful in this generation. They have supported us during the mountain top and the valley low experiences of our lives. They have been donors to Women of Vision and Destiny Ministries, Inc, and investors in our dreams. We are eternally grateful for you.

WHAT OTHERS ARE SAYING

God said you (L. Renee) been released into the earth

For such a time as this. Women (and men)

are going to now see the manifestation of their

calling through your teaching and training.

The witty ideas inside you will bring forth much

fruit through the lives of many. Think it

not strange that you will give someone an idea

and if they implement it within 24 hours they

will become rich.

KIM CRAWFORD, CEO

CONTENTS

1 LIVE DEBT FREE

Now there cried a certain woman of the wives of the sons of the prophets unto Elisha, saying, Thy servant my husband is dead: and thou knowest that thy servant did fear the Lord and the creditor is come to take unto him my two sons to be bondmen. 2 Kings 4:1

The curtain opens in the fourth chapter of the second book of Kings in the Bible. We are introduced to the painful cries of a widow woman who is frantic about her financial situation. Her husband was a prophet or a seer. He was called by God to see into the future and let people know what was on their horizon. The scene opens after his death and what we see is heart wrenching. The prophet worked for years serving God and His people. He died and left his family in a horrific financial situation. They were broke, headed to bankruptcy court and the collateral that was going to be taken was both of the widow's sons.

The creditor had to earn his money back and her sons would become the assets for their father's debt. We can only wonder did the prophet see this day coming. His debt would now cost the sacrifice of his own sons. We are blessed to live in America. Our creditors can take our assets (homes, cars, equipment) but they are not allowed to take our bodies or our children.

The story is interrupting in that it shows us that you can be God fearing and yet make unwise financial decisions that put you heavily in debt. The prophet was clearly a servant of God but he made financial decisions that had a huge impact on his future generations. At his funeral, his family mourned his passing and sat in fear, thinking about what life was going to hold for them when they got home. Perhaps they had seen the collection notices stamped in red signifying the urgency of payment. Perhaps they saw the notices saying utilities were scheduled to be shut off. Their situation was bleak.

You can be a servant of the Lord and make poor financial decisions. The Bible says my people are destroyed for lack of knowledge. Hosea 4:5. Yes, it says a Christian's lack of Wealth and Riches™ knowledge can destroy him or her. Poor financial understanding also impacts generations. The creditor is coming for her sons – to take them to work off the debt that their father owed. The Bible is true when it says the borrower is servant to the lender in Proverbs 22:7. Her sons were going to become slaves for their father's debt. The Bible is silent on how much debt the prophet owed. The amount is irrelevant. One person can owe $1,000 and another can owe $100,000. Both can be on the verge of bankruptcy. The cause of the indebtness is irrelevant too. Medical bills, business loans, excess living, job loss can all contribute to a household's financial dilemma.

First, the widow lost her husband. Now the creditor was coming to take her two sons. The loss of her entire family was too much for her to bear. Enough is enough, she thought. In her desperation, she made a critical decision to take back her God-given power over her life. She decided to not settle for the hand that life had dealt her. She decided to do something to change her circumstances.

This is the critical ingredient of the *haves* vs. the *have nots*. Jesus exhorted in three different gospels, to him who has will be given abundance, to him who has not that which he has will be taken away. Most of us equate *having* and *having not* only with money. I believe that money is easy to produce but Wealth and Riches™ comes from within. It is the external manifestation of the value that we create on the inside of us. God calls it *wealth and riches* in Psalms 112. It's a promise to the child of God.

Have people pull from deep within their spirit and begin to tap a reservoir of faith that changes the trajectory of their destiny. They decide to no longer be broke, depressed, trodden down, and overlooked. They take action steps that propel them to success. Once they get to another level of success, they aim even higher. *Have* people are like the four lepers in second Kings the seventh chapter who decide it is better to enter the enemy's camp than to stay in a land under siege and die. Little did these lepers know that the sounds of their feet would frighten the enemy away. Faith steps go a long way. We must do something about our situation. Moving forward unlocks destinies. Keep moving and things will happen. Most of the world's self made millionaires were flat broke and made a decision to turn their life around by taking Wealth and Riches Action Steps™.

Have not people give up and decide to throw in the towel. Life cannot get any worse they think. Life is too much. I cannot go on. With this vision of their lives, the *have nots* give up.

The prophet's wife had a powerful *have* character strength—she did not give up despite the bleakness of her situation. The widow had the wisdom to contact the man of God for help. The Bible says "who can find a virtuous woman?" Proverbs 31:10. Virtue is the same word associated with wealth. Wealth comes from the Hebrew word chayil which means force, strength, army and activity.

The dead prophet had great insight when he selected his wife. One of the greatest financial decisions a man will make is the selection of his wife. "Whoso findeth a wife

findeth a good thing, and obtaineth favour of the LORD."
Proverbs 18:22. Favour is the divine goodwill which God
extends to humanity as He sees fit. The writer does not
give us insight into the prophet's wife or why he chose her.
I believe she was a Proverbs wife. "A virtuous woman is a
crown to her husband." Proverbs 12:4 Her price is far
above rubies. Proverbs 31:10.

During the earlier centuries rubies were considered
more valuable than diamonds. In the 16th century rubies
were priced eight times higher than other stones. Imagine
their worth during Bible times. No wonder the Proverbs 31
writer, who was a woman, exclaimed, who can find her?

A natural ruby has imperfections. What were the
widow's imperfections? Did she leave household financial
decisions totally to her husband? Was she unaware of his
financial dealings? Was she shocked when she got the
letter from the creditor saying her husband owed more

than he could pay? The price tag for the balance due was to be the loss of her sons. Did the creditors send her a notice giving her a deadline for her sons to be picked up? She had the wisdom to cry out with the expectation that the man of God had an answer that would change her Present Financial Status™(PFS).

We can follow her example and use our faith, build a plan and work your plan until it yields the desired results. Her plan was simple. Get an advisor. In the multitude of counsel, there is safety according to Proverbs 15:22.

Wealth and Riches™ Affirmation

He who walketh with wise men shall be wise; but the companion

of fools shall be destroyed. Proverbs 13:20

2 DISCOVER WHAT'S IN YOUR HOUSE?

And Elisha said unto her, What shall I do for thee? Tell me, what

hast thou in the house? And she said, Thine handmaid hath not

anything in the house… 2 Kings 4:2

The widow approached her husband's leader with the expectation of favorable results. It is important to note that the prophet Elijah did not condemn her household's past financial mistakes. She was already under the condemnation of too much debt. We know the feeling when we see our credit card bills and think how did this bill become this high? Many of us beat ourselves up for financial decisions that did not turn out favorable. This belief keeps us under condemnation and fear. Fear immobilizes us from moving forward and taking the Wealth and Riches Action Plan™ to set us free. Let's not wallow in condemnation and self unforgiveness. Repent and move forward.

The man of God provided a solution that made her the central figure to her own deliverance. He basically said, I am not your solution. The answer lies within you. He points out that the solution to her Wealth and Riches™ woes were already in her house. She has the gold that needs to be mined right under her nose. The widow's situation was desperate. How could the answer lie within her house? She thought she had nothing left to give. I do not have *anything* in the house, she thought.

The prophet's question pulled on the strings of her imagination. Did he know something that she did not know? What could he see? What could it be? It takes a tremendous amount of soul searching to discover the answer. During dark economic seasons many people believe that they have nothing left to give. We are instructed to ask, and it will be given to you. Seek and you will find. Knock and the door will be opened to you. Matthew 7:7. It is when we begin to dig deeper that the answers come. We have to believe that within us are the seeds of greatness that God planted to turn our circumstances around. We all have them. It is according to how we believe and our ability to cultivate these seeds of faith.

As the widow searched for contents of value in her home, she finally had the insight to mention the only thing of value to her. After stretching her brain to think of something, the widow replied that she had *nothing. Thine handmaid hath not anything in the house.*

The item was so insignificant she considered it nothing.

What are the *nothings* that are in our lives that we overlook? We talk ourselves out of their importance. We consider them minute and trivial. Combined with faith and a determination to ask, seek, and knock we can create a snowball effect that will change our lives and the lives of our children.

It is easy to put ourselves, life experiences and skills in a bucket of *nothing*. We believe we went to school and got the *nothing* degree. We could have majored in something else. We married a *nothing* guy and had a *nothing* child and live in a *nothing* neighborhood and drive a *nothing* car. The problem is not that we have nothing, it is that we *see* nothing. Our vision is blurred by life's challenges. The struggles have left us beaten down, depressed, oppressed and hopeless. We have given up on our lives and settled for the mundane and ordinary.

Our lives are designed to be full and abundant. We

have all been designed to play the beautiful music that the Master has placed within us. When the music dies, we die emotionally, mentally, and eventually physically. Life without purpose and hope is meaningless. Who wants to get out of bed and look out the window when our mind plays our failures over and over again. Woulda, coulda, shoulda's stare us in the face and mock our efforts to move forward. You failed. You knew better. Everyone is laughing at you.

We put our hands over our ears to shut the voices out. The widow shut her voices out when she focused on answering the prophet's question, "Tell me, what you have in the house?" The question ripped through her doubt and fear and it pulled her out of the darkness of her pain and despair. If the prophet can see it, so can I.

She began her own soul searching. What is in me that will produce my Wealth and Riches™? How can I be the solution to my own problem?

It is the same question Jesus asked when he had 4,000 souls to feed in a desert. There were no restaurants, catering companies, Wal-Mart's or Costco's in the desert. Jesus asked, How many loaves do you have? Mark 8:5.

In order for Christ to work in our lives to produce Wealth and Riches™, we must first ... *have*! This is a kingdom secret. It's a small but very significant principle that changes the future of your life. Jesus needs a seed from us. His system requires faith and a seed to yield its riches.

If you have made mistakes, it is best to repent of financial mistakes and move forward. Do not dwell in condemnation. Jesus did not come to condemn us but to save us from our failures or life lessons. Failure is a course in what not to do again or gives us lessons on what to do better next time.

WEALTH AND RICHES™ LIFE APPLICATION

What are some financial mistakes you have made?

_____

_____

_____

_____

Name some changes you are going to do immediately to begin your Wealth and Riches™ journey. The choice is yours. Today is the day.

_____

_____

_____

_____

_____

_____

_____

To become our own solution to our Wealth and Riches™

problems, we must search our houses. What things of value

are in your house? _____

_____

_____

_____

Wealth and Riches™ Affirmation

Psalm 112:1-3

Praise ye the LORD, Blessed is the man that feareth

the LORD, that delighteth greatly in his

commandments. His seed shall be mighty upon the

earth; the generation of the upright shall be blessed.

Wealth and riches shall be in his house: and his

righteousness endureth forever.

3 OVERCOME FEAR WITH COURAGE

For God hath not given us the spirit of fear; but of power, and of love,

and of a sound mind. 2 Timothy 1:7

The widow had to address thoughts of fear that were swirling in her mind. She had to deal with her thoughts of fear and terror and the possibility of losing her sons. We must address and acknowledge our fears. Then we must use the word of God to destroy them again and again until they dissipate.

We must deal with the thoughts that do not align with the word of God and replace them with God inspired thoughts. When you experience extreme seasons of uncertainty, fear comes in and sets up a room in your mental home. The more we feed fear, the more space it takes over in our minds. When fear comes in, it immobilizes our ability to move forward and take the steps to turn our situation around. God has not given us the spirit of fear. So the question remains, where did it come from? Who gave it to you? In Genesis 3:10, after Adam sinned, he stated that "I was afraid" and hid himself. It's in our human genes to be afraid and hide ourselves. Jesus says do not be afraid, only believe Luke 8:50.

We hide our gifts and talents after we experience a failure or a setback. If we interview for a job and make it to round three but do not get selected, fear comes in and takes over space in our mind. It tells us do not try again. Fear says you will get all the way to the final round and lose again. Do not try again, fear whispers. These become our self-limiting beliefs.

If we lose our jobs or homes, the enemy tells us that we were not worthy of that job or you did not deserve that home. See, look what happened, fear whispers. That's the voice of fear and it gains more and more power and room in our mental homes as we experience the obstacles of life.

So how do we get rid of fear? Real simple, we open the door of our mind and replace words of fear with words of faith. We throw out the rubbish that fear has placed in our minds. We change the voice of fear into the voice of courage. When fear says you can't, courage replies, yes, I can. Some of our mental rooms are full of fear's cobwebs of past experiences that did not work out. When new opportunities come up, fear says no. Fear says it's better to never try again than to try again and lose. Not true.

Courage says keep trying because one day the results are going to be different. Courage says you may walk into

100 closed doors, but on the 101st time, somebody is going to let you in! Courage says do not give up until you see the results that God has promised you. We must embrace the promises of God. God told Joshua, do not be afraid, be courageous.

Wealth and Riches™ building takes courage and activity. Courage is the quality of mind or spirit that enables a person to face difficulty without fear or do it in spite of fear. We can face any financial decisions we need to make today. We can look for new careers that bring in more wealth. We can change cities to live our dreams. We can deal with creditors and walk through the valley of bankruptcy without fearing any evil. Why? Because if you are His child, all things are possible to him who believes.

We can make years of mistakes and get back on the right track. The widow woman tapped into a kingdom secret. Her husband was God's servant and feared the

Lord. I believe the dead prophet paid his tithes and offerings faithfully, giving his ten percent of his increase to the temple. His future was protected by his past giving. I believe that we have two bank accounts: our earthly one and our heavenly one. One pays in interest, the kingdom pays in folds. Some thirty, sixty and hundred fold (Mark 10:31), which is much greater than one percent interest a year. God's system works. He told us to "prove Him" in Malachi 3:10.

We can develop a new Wealth and Riches™ mindset and live by spiritually responsible guidelines. The Hebrew word for wealth is chayil which means force, strength, army, activity. Chayil is also the same word used to describe the Proverbs 31 woman. Wealth and Riches® will not fall into our laps. He gives us the power to get wealth and we must use it. We must develop a systematic "Wealth and Riches Action Plan™" to achieve our success.

Faith must be accompanied by works. The definition of Biblical wealth means an army, letting us know it will require a team of people to make your dreams come true. We need God's strength to stay in faith during the lean years when we are planting seeds but not seeing any increase. All businesses and individuals go through lean cow years of famine and dire circumstances, typically followed by fat cow years of tremendous abundance. In the Genesis 47:26 , Joseph's system of saving twenty percent during the fat cow years, saved the entire planet and the Jewish nation.

In the first book of Kings and the eighteenth chapter, Elijah had prayed that the heavens would be shut up and the showers from heaven stopped. At his words, the heavens listened and it did not rain for three and a half years. When he prayed for rain again, Elijah took his servant to the top of the mountain and told the servant to look toward the sea, while Elijah kneeled down and put his face between his knees 2 Kings 18: 42. Elijah was looking for a sign that his prayer for rain had been answered. The servant kept coming back to Elijah saying that he saw *nothing.*

Elijah kept sending the servant back to look for the sign that it was going to rain. Finally, after seven trips, the servant said all I see is a *cloud* the size of a man's hand. Look at your hand. I just wonder how the servant was able to see such a small, insignificant hand sized *cloud* way up in the sky. Certainly the servant thought, this is *nothing* important. It's going to take a lot more than a *cloud the size of a man's hand* to do something to replenish this drought. The grounds are brown with ruined foliage. The bark on the trees is lifeless. The animals are famished from not having enough pasture to feed on. The servant mentioned the little cloud to Elijah. The prophet Elijah knew that the little cloud was the answer to his prayer. He told his servant to go and tell the king to get ready to get down before the torrential rain poured down. It was going to rain so hard that the king would be stopped from coming down the mountain.

We have to look not just for the job interview but for the *little cloud* of resume writing, calling the human resources department, networking with people from the company and applying over and over again for our dream career. These are our little clouds. Little clouds produce the sounds of the abundance of rain when we mix our prayer requests with faith. Go. Keep moving. Your prayers are on the verge of being answered. This revelation comes when we bind the spirit of fear and unleash the power of courage.

Mental re-programming begins with an examination of our thoughts. As I began my quest from a dark place in my life, I discovered that to change my outcome or the results that I was seeing in my life, I had to change my thinking. This revelation said that my thoughts were driving the results that I saw in my physical world. When we begin to re-shape our lives, the first thing that has to been cleaned up is our thoughts. What are we thinking about all the time?

During a dark season, my thoughts were not positive. Our dream Michigan Avenue ice cream business closed after six years. We had invested our savings in this franchise. A few months later, the Lord blessed my husband with a new job. We were excited. The future looked bright. Three months later, he had a cerebral hemorrhage that left him hospitalized for five weeks. At one point in my life, my thoughts were consumed with darkness and fear. Needless to say that's what I kept experiencing. I had to work to replace my thoughts with the words of God that created abundance.

Our household had more that was scheduled to go out than the income that was coming in. This produced a great amount of fear because I had never been here before. Life was challenging. We learned to live by faith.

I started a job with the dream of building a new career. My goal was to go in as a managerial trainee and become a district manager overseeing multiple stores to motivate, empower and inspire women's leaders to achieve incredible results. I figured that if I could run our own store, I could run someone else's business. I had learned a tremendous amount about store operations. The pay was less than ideal but it was full time and offered benefits and opportunity for advancement or so I thought.

I picked my ideal company that I loved and was passionate about. Three years later, I was stuck in a dead end position with little signs of advancement. However, it was in this setting that I re-discovered my purpose and began to coach women who worked with me. These ladies had entrepreneurial dreams. My corporate and business ownership experiences could provide insight into their dreams.

Wealth and Riches™ became a promise to my husband and me. We were walking by faith and it was a tough time. God's word was my comfort and courage. I began to tackle thoughts of fear and replace them with God's words of courage.

Every day and throughout the day, I meditated on God's words and promises. His word became more and more real to me. My vision and thoughts began to shift to abundance and hope.

Wealth and Riches™ Affirmation

I counsel thee to buy of me gold tried in the fire, that thou mayest be rich; and white raiment, that thou mayest be clothed, and that the shame of thy nakedness do not appear; and anoint thane eyes with

eyesalve, that thou mayest see. Revelations 3:18

Wealth and Riches™ Promises

What are some of your favorite scriptures that God has promised

you and your house?

_____

_____

_____

_____

_____

_____

_____

_____

4 REBUILD YOUR MIND WITH THE WORD

Praise ye the LORD, blessed is the man that feareth the LORD that delighteth greatly in his commandments. Psalm 112:1

Fear was instilling negative ideas in my mind. I had to build up my courage. I knew God's word was the key. My mom always quoted a scripture that said the seed of the righteous shall be delivered. I thought she said it was found in Psalm 112. So finally after hearing it so much, I decided to read the passage of scripture.

Praise ye the LORD, blessed is the man that feareth the LORD that delighteth greatly in his commandments. His seed shall be mighty upon the earth; the generation of the upright shall be blessed. Wealth and riches shall be in his house; and his righteousness endureth forever. Psalm 112:1-3. These words of the promise of Wealth and Riches™ rang out in my spirit like the liberty bell. I grabbed the promise of God and held on to it like a drowning man holds on to a rope. These words breathed life into my soul. Wealth and Riches™. Wealth and Riches™. It became my platform and eventually the new the name of my company, Wealth & Riches Today, Inc.

During this season of extreme darkness, I connected with D. Michelle Thompson on the phone one night and began to do what I always do…mentor and coach. As I was listening to myself on the call, I heard these words, physician, heal thyself found in Luke 4:23. I felt the Lord was saying to me, you have what it takes to change your life already inside of you. You have always coached and mentored others, do the same for yourself. Speak to yourself. I am so glad I listened to this voice.

Darice is a powerful business woman who left corporate America just like me to live her dreams. She birthed Designed for Destiny and published a great book Table for One, Please! for singles (www.tablefor1.org). I was always amazed at how brilliant she was. She held a book signing at our Michigan Avenue ice cream store. Now life had gone through swift transitions for the both of us.

I felt like Dorothy from the Wizard of Oz. Just click your heels and go home. What we are searching for was already inside of us. Darice and I agreed to meet once a week to coordinate our efforts. So Darice and I partnered for success and brainstormed about creating a two-part tele-seminar series on Sunday nights. I would teach us how to discover our untapped Wealth and Riches™ and she would teach us to become authors. Her program was called ACTS based on Acts 1:8 and stood for Authors

Coached to Succeed. She scheduled her call early in the early evening. I could be on her call in my car going home from work. Since I worked in retail, working weekends was part of the assignment. I picked the only time that I knew that I would have free---Sunday evenings at 8 p.m. I always said, I will own my time again one day real soon. We can speak to our circumstances.

I created a platform that began as a monthly women's tele-seminar called Wealth and Riches™ are in my House based on Psalm 112. It was designed for women who had hit major roadblocks in their lives and wanted to be coached and mentored back to financial success. The monthly fee would be $6.95 a month, an extremely affordable price. The goal of the tele-seminar was to guide us through credit restoration, divorce recovery, job loss, foreclosure, bankruptcy and life health challenges. It would be a sanctuary for women to support and encourage each other during the worse economic period since the great depression.

I was walking in fear when I sent out an email announcing the new tele-seminar to my Women of Vision and Destiny, Inc. network. I was afraid to see if people responded. Finally a few weeks later, I was at a woman's event and a lady came over and said she saw my email and wanted to sign up for the program. I was dumbfounded. Yes, I know it sounds crazy but when you walk in fear, you are surprised when people respond positively. Hearing her words breathed life into my idea. I went back to my emails finally and saw that a few women were very interested as well. Courage stood up and said there is something to this concept. Courage began to ignite my thoughts in a new direction of…Yes, I can. I sent a text to our church's Sunday School superintendent's wife about teaching an elective course called Wealth and Riches™ are in My

House based on the revelations I received from Psalm 112.

The four week series was designed to empower students with Biblical and financial tools to put them on a solid financial future. I did the unbelievable for me at that time; I put a price tag on it. To charge for my services was a huge step. I was a philanthropist and loved to give. I felt I heard in my spirit, do not do it for free. I could give extreme discounts but free was not an option.

It was a huge thinking change for me. My husband and I and a group of dedicated women had built a women's organization, Women of Vision and Destiny, Inc. We used our personal wealth, and the donations from board members, partners, and friends. We gave away over eight hundred Women of Destiny Bibles and hosted over one hundred events (workshops, conferences, and Bible studies) for nearly fifteen years. We did not charge the women to come but depended on donations. My husband

and I poured thousands of our own money into the ministry. Women like Ernestine Carter, Vernetta Wisniewski, Geneva Edwards, Maisie Sparks, and my parents poured time, money, and energy into our programs.

Being obedient to the idea that I came to me, I asked that the Sunday School to charge $20 for two people to attend to cover materials. I took the time off from my work for the four weeks. On the first day of class, only one student had showed up and the class was scheduled to be cancelled. One of my faithful Sunday School supporters stood up and made a convincing announcement and explained that the course was two for $20. Finally I had enough students for the class to begin. Every week more and more people heard about the class signed up and came.

During one of my sessions, a student told me that people get paid $25,000 a day for what I was teaching. I was shocked. I asked him if I could pay him to coach me on how to become a coach at this major company. So for about fifteen to twenty minutes after each class, he designed a strategy for me. I followed his advice and soon I had an offer to become a coach for this multi-million dollar company.

I had to create materials for the Sunday School course. Given my hectic schedule, each week I wrote one chapter for my class handouts. This teaching assignment forced me to write again. My first chapter was on the widow woman in second Kings and is now the foundation for this book. I began to practice the Wealth and Riches™ principles that I wrote about and my life began to change.

I read a study that said only 1.8% of women businesses made over $1 million a year. Most of women businesses earn less than $10,000, the report stated. My company, Leap of Faith University LLC, created a goal of increasing the number of women businesses that earn over $1 million a year including myself. Leap of Faith University, LLC has since been renamed to Wealth and Riches Today, Inc.™

It was during this class that my students began to pull greatness out of me. They asked for a coaching program to help ordinary people navigate life. These students told me that information I was giving was so powerful and that I should charge more.

Many of my students would walk up to me and bless me with money. I was stunned but I knew what was going on. I was walking in my true calling. My purpose involves teaching others how to produce their Wealth and Riches™ by finding their true calling. It's built on walking by faith until the wealth materializes. Never give up!

I began to de-program my mind with a book that I already had in my home. I had purchased the book twelve months earlier but had not read it or put it to action.

The book was by my fabulous mentor, Cheryl

Broussard, who wrote *Sister CEO*. The book is the *Sister CEO Guide to the Law of Attraction, Creating Financial Abundance to Live the Life of Your Dreams*. Ms. Broussard spoke at our 2011 International Christian Women's Conference sponsored by Women of Vision and Destiny, Inc.

I purchased her E-book and it was emailed to me. I actually printed it out. I acted upon the book and began to enlarge my mind. My mind was hit hard by life's circumstances.

I would spend fifteen minutes during my lunch break building my Wealth and Riches Action Plan™ for my company and increasing my faith. I knew in Christ there had to be a place of peace. He provided shelter in my storm.

5 DE-CLUTTER YOUR LIFE

"And Elisha said unto her, What shall I do for thee? Tell me, what

hast thou in the house? 2 Kings 4:2

Once I replaced fear with courage, I could begin to focus

on my external world. The external world is a reflection of

the inner world. If someone asks you what's in your house,

how would you respond? We are blessed to live in a 4,000

square feet home with four bedrooms, three and half

bathrooms, a den, a family room and a four level platform.

I can look over and see three different levels at one time.

We have been in our house sixteen years and have lived the

American Dream of accumulation. Just today I found a cleaning instrument that I forgot I had. I also found a ministry tool that I have never used. I kept discovering new things in my own home. I also discovered my dreams that were in Dream Files, waiting for the vision to speak. Habakkuk 2:2 tells us to write the vision and make it plain upon tables, that he may run that readeth it.

To answer prophet Elijah's question of what do I have in my house, I would have to visit each room in my house and review its contents, especially those of the huge closets on the lower level. We have tons of closets that housed our home, businesses and non-profit organizations files. A plumbing incident left these files sprawled on upper levels while repair and restoration was performed in the lower level.

While I believe I did not buy a lot of extra things, living itself lends to accumulation. Most of us take in but we do not throw out or give away. America is a nation of storage centers. The growth of storage centers has grown tremendously over the last ten years.

Storage centers are on every other mile alluring us with their free first month's rent. Our stuff is now so important that we have Container Stores to help us store our stuff. We have TV shows that talk about people's obsession with stuff that they hoard. We pay rent or mortgages on our first property and then fork over another $200-$300 a month to store our extra stuff. Throwing these things out is not an option. We must hold on to them, we believe. Our bathrooms are littered with stuff we no longer use. Our cabinets and drawers house our old products that are almost empty. Our garages are littered with empty bottles and bags and old cars we do not drive. It is hard for Americans to let go of things.

Have you ever drove by a garage sale and said, I can't

believe that they are selling that stuff. Yes, and people come and buy another man's old stuff. We have more and more stuff. We convince ourselves that we do not want to waste anything so we save it. It would be nice if we were diligent about saving our money.

Most of this stuff is stuff that we will never use but are emotionally attached to it. Old T-shirts, old clothes we wore in high school, old cars, old grills, old pots, old dishes, old tableware, old sheets, old towels. As we age, we find it even harder to throw away our stuff.

Hence our issues. We have become a nation of accumulators and therefore are often unaware of all of the things we have. We do not conduct annual inventories because our stuff is not attached to revenue. It's just stuff. Stuff to be put in a closet, stuff to be put in a container under the bed or over the refrigerator. Every nook and cranny is filled with stuff.

I wonder did the widow woman have the same problem. Did she have to mentally go through every room in her house to think of what she had in her home? Or did the simplicity of life back then make it much easier for her to let the prophet know what was in her house.

I use a Bible based organization system for my clients. It's based on *D.O.P.S.S.* It stands for *De-Clutter, Organize, Prioritize, Schedule and Sacrifice.*

De-clutter your life. Start with your workspace in your home—the birthing place of your dreams. Wealth and Riches™ comes to places that are uncluttered and organized. Simplify your personal space. Make your office a sanctuary.

Look at your desk, eliminate the clutter. Buy file folders and create an alphabetized system for filing. Clean up your emails and organize them in folders. Having 5,000 emails in your inbox creates clutter and dilutes your ability to attract Wealth and Riches™. Delete the voice mails and text messages on your cell phone. You will feel a huge level of accomplishment when you clean up your emails and voicemails.

Visit your car, clean it out. You are a reflection of your personal brand. Clean out the trunk and keep it clean. Clutter comes easily and takes away your energy and ability to focus. Open your closet and give away all of the items that you have not worn in the last twelve months...especially the items you plan to wear when you lose weight. Your bedroom is a reflection of your mind. Keep it clutter free. Hang up your clothes when you take them off. Delaying to do so results in clutter. Visit your bathroom and clean out old items that you no longer use.

There will be people in your life who you will need to minimize contact with and ultimately delete from your timeline. Look for new circles with like minded individuals who want to make a difference in the world. Let some things die...bad habits, bad thoughts, and bad relationships.

Organize your life. Build your business and dream around a relationship with God. Launch a daily devotional and Bible Study time. I prefer structured twelve month programs filled with the meditation, memorization of scriptures and based on the promises of God (www.mastersline.com). These promises can go on your walls in your office in nice picture frames.

What is God's purpose for your life? Design your vision to meet His purpose. Get a notebook and keep it with you at all times. Write down your thoughts. Get a good study Bible and notebook. Spend time with God and ask Him about your life. He will answer. Ask him to give you the wisdom to build your business and dreams.

If you are over involved in your church, council or

national organization, cut back any over commitments. Something is most likely not getting done. Volunteer for one spot and be faithful. One thing at a time. *Organize* your purse, wallet, and wardrobe. Clean the paper clutter out of your wallet on a daily basis. Color Code your life (Use colored folders for each entity e.g.. Home-Red. Business-Blue. Ministry-Pink.)

Wealth and Riches™ Affirmation

He becometh poor that dealeth with a slack hand: but the hand of the diligent maketh rich. Proverbs 10:4

Wealth and Riches™ Action Plan

I will de-clutter the following areas of my life in the next 90 days.

_____

_____

_____

6 MASTER TIME MANAGEMENT

So teach us to number our days, that we may apply our hearts

unto wisdom. Psalm 90:12

Wealth and Riches™ creation is an incredible power. It comes with a great deal of responsibility. It will require every essence of your being. Many people give up before seeing manifestation of their dreams. Dreamers need two great skills to deliver the greatness that lies within: time or self management and prioritization. It is important to manage one's time and learn the secret of *prioritization*. A powerful time manager has mastered two secret ingredients: focus and concentration. Focus is the ability to pursue a project with the intensity to get it done. Concentration is the ability to reach one hundred percent completion.

Minimize or totally stop multi-tasking. Focus and concentrate on one thing at a time. It is important to prioritize, make the *first* things *first*. Time is spent. Do not spend it unwisely. Matthew 6:33 says, seek ye first the kingdom of God and his righteousness and all these things shall be added unto you.

Prioritization is the discipline of knowing that to do first and when to move on to the next most important thing on the list. To prioritize, go in order of importance. When you start your day, ask yourself what is the most important thing I need to do today? What is the vision for my life? Is this activity going to take me closer to my vision. Make a list. What are the three biggest things I need to accomplish today? Start with the most important task and complete it first. Do not move to the next one on the list until the most important is completed. Learn to say yes or no. Work on participating in activities that help you focus on your goals. Be willing to cut the smart phones completely off for periods of time. I have learned that it is sometimes easier to just leave the phone in another room. Do not check emails or phone messages or text continually. Schedule email and phone times like you schedule a meeting.

Say No...Politely but firmly. Decide if you need to participate or delegate. Decide if the project needs to be completed now or later.

It is better to live a plated life versus a buffet life. A plated life has space between portions or priorities. A buffet life is overstuffed with too many items on the plate. Save your money and time. We have 24 hours a day, 168 hours in a week and 611,520 hours in an average lifetime.

Scheduling is the art of allotting a time space to work on opportunities. It requires that we write our activities down. The shortest pencil is longer than your memory. God was organized and days were scheduled.

Let's look at creation. God designed seven days to fit in a week. Tuesday always follows Monday. We have 30 or 31 days in a month, except February. February always follows January. 365(6) days in a year. Years go up in number not down. Time must be used wisely. It can never be used again.

Invest in a good calendar. Visit an office supply store in July and purchase your calendar for the upcoming year. Your calendar needs to show: three years at a glance, twelve months at a glance, a month at a glance, a week at a glance and days broken down into hourly detail. A place in the calendar is needed for notes for the year, month, week and day. While many people use a computerized calendar, There is something incredibly powerful about a portable calendar book. In July of each year, lay out your calendar for the next year.

Set goals for an annual, quarterly, monthly, weekly and daily period of time. Your goals are the pathways to success. You may have heard of building S.M.A.R.T. Goals. They are Specific. Measurable. Achievable. Realistic. Timely.

Three are two basic time lengths for goals. Short-Term goals are five years or less. Long term goals are five years or longer. Time goes by so fast. You can do more in ten years than you can imagine. Successful people are planning three to ten years ahead. To reach your goals, start with the longest time period and break it down into smaller pieces. For example, start with a twelve month goal and break it down into four 90 day periods. Focus on the 90 days and then break them down into 30 day goals. Always have a contingency plan. Re-evaluate your goals in light of your life every day.

The most important question remains. Are you ready to live the *sacrificial* life? Are you willing to make the sacrifices that lead to success?

Wealth and Riches™ Action Plan

_____

_____

_____

_____

_____

_____

_____

_____

_____

7 GROW YOUR POT OF OIL

"And she said, thine handmaid hath not any thing in her house, save

a pot of oil." 2 Kings 4:2b

The widow came to the man of God expecting to receive

help. Her husband worked for the prophet. She believed

the prophet Elijah had the answer to her situation. Elijah's

next question was life changing. He was pointing her in a

new direction. His response was, "what do you have in

your house?" All of the answers to our questions come

from deep within us. We learned that we have to have

something or a seed to reap abundance. His next question was life changing. What shall I do for you? He was pointing her in a new direction. He knew the answer was within her own power.

The widow replied, all that she had was a pot of oil I believe that God places a pot of oil inside of each of us. It's our YOU-uniqueness® combined with our life experiences and ability to learn new things that will produce our wealth. When you have walked through the valley of the *shadow* of financial death, all you tend to see is evil. The scripture (Psalms 23) points out that it is just a shadow of death and not the real deal. The secret is to deal with the fear and proclaim, I will fear no evil.

The first step we must take is to spend more time understanding who we are and how did God create us to be You-nique®? Mankind is created like the snowflake— no two individuals are alike. All of us are different and created with the designer's purpose. We must understand that God desires for us to trust Him and commit our resources to His use.

I meet so many people who follow the American Dream for their lives. They go to school, get an education, get a six figure job and live the good life as the world defines it. I was one of them. Yet research shows that about seventy percent of people hate their jobs and dream of doing something different, but they are afraid to take their pot of oil and do something with it.

The pot of oil did not become important until the prophet asked the widow, what is in your house?. It only became crucial because all else has failed. This is why we see that many of today's self-made millionaires were single or divorced moms with kids who had to create ideas to generate Wealth and Riches™ to feed their kids and survive a tough season in their lives. They rose up to the occasion. They searched for the pot of oil that will produce revenue. It's this deep soul searching that Wealth and Riches™ are birthed.

Finding your pot of oil or true calling comes from spending one of the most powerful assets that we have – time with God and ourselves. We are members of a global community. We also need to spend time with others. To discover your purpose or find the pot of oil that's in your house, will require you to spend solitary time with God. We have to build seasons of quiet time with God and ourselves to create the greatest masterpieces and blueprints for our lives.

One of my good friends has built a mission to get the busy man and woman to spend quality and quantity time with God. She invites us to come away and spend contemplative time with God. She hosts the most powerful retreats where we come away and spend time with

God and journal. These soul searching one day events replace months of busy time and we get the answers to so many of our questions. Jesus was a master at spending quality time with God.

We see Him spending solitary moments away from the masses that pressed against Him looking for their miracles. He would spend time with God alone and private time with His disciples. Greatness is in all of us and there is plenty of Wealth and Riches™ for each of us. The Word of God re-builds. I purchased labels that said Wealth and Riches™ shall be in his house and placed them everywhere. My mom would always call me and tell me these great words…stay in faith.

My You-uniqueness™ is designed to complement not compete with yours. Let's take a moment to understand ourselves and how we can produce wealth.

Wealth and Riches™ Affirmation

Riches and honour are with me: yea, durable riches and righteousness. My fruit is better than fine gold; and my revenue than choice silver. Proverbs 8:18-19

Wealth and Riches™ Toolkit – An Inventory of My Life It's been said that your mess is your message. Your pain is your purpose. What setbacks have you overcome in life?

_____

_____

_____

_____

_____

What career(s) have you been most successful at?

_____

If you could start your life all over again, what career would you go into? What's holding you back now?

_____

_____

_____

_____

What skills have you mastered? Are people are willing to pay for your knowledge?

_____

_____

_____

_____

What skills do you have that you define as a hobby and you enjoy sharing these skills for free?

_____

_____

What do people always ask you about or look to you for

expertise?_____

_____

_____

_____

_____

_____

_____

Who can you partner with? Who else loves to do what you

do?

_____

_____

_____

_____

_____

What are you really passionate about and would love to do the rest of your life?

_____

_____

_____

_____

_____

_____

What areas are you passionate about? Can you become an expert in that area?

_____

_____

_____

_____

_____

What special knowledge do you have that others would like

to know?

_____

_____

_____

_____

_____

_____

What subjects interest you the most?

_____

_____

_____

_____

_____

_____

What are your hobbies? How many hours a week/month do you spend on these activities? Are other people getting paid to do what you love to do?

_____

_____

_____

_____

List the jobs you held and the companies that you worked for that you enjoyed the most. What were the industries?

_____

_____

_____

_____

_____

Make a list of awards you have received over the years.

_____

_____

_____

_____

_____

_____

What professional groups do you belong to? What

positions do you hold in these groups? What groups do you

want to network with?

_____

_____

_____

_____

What categories of magazines do you enjoy reading?

_____

_____

_____

What skills/natural talents do you have?

_____

_____

_____

What areas of your expertise can be turned into a book, a

CD, a video, a blog, a workshop, or a speaking

engagement, an event a bootcamp or specialized training?

_____

_____

_____

_____

Are you an experienced user of Microsoft Office or an accounting software? Which ones? Are you an expert? Can you teach others to use the systems?

_____

_____

_____

_____

_____

_____

What social media tools do you optimize and can teach others about?

_____

_____

_____

_____

_____

What automated systems do you know? (e.g. Eventbrite, Blogging, GoDaddy, Paypal, etc.)

_____

_____

_____

_____

_____

The secret to building your expertise is **Wealth and Riches™ Continuous Learning**. Take classes, read books, attend conferences, network with others in your field. These steps will boost your knowledge, confidence and visibility.

What classes can you take to certify your knowledge? Visit the local colleges in your area and look for certifications programs. Jesus was seen at age twelve in the temple with the wisest religious scholars at that time.

Surround yourself with the industry's best and brightest.

Next you must position yourself as the expert. Teach classes at a local library, church or community organizations. Develop the content, create a professional flyer and send out to your friends and family. Then invite groups of people who may not know you. Do not worry about who or how many people attend, you are building your expertise in this area. Develop a professional photo and bio promoting your experiences, training and expertise. Create a brochure or a one-sheeter on you and your services. The key is to get moving knowing who you are becoming and what you have to offer the greater society. You were put here to serve the world. Do it. Do not be ashamed to be great. God made you that way.

Building your Wealth an Riches® Toolbox comes with understanding who you are and what expertise you have that others will pay you for. I meet so many potential millionaires who are stuck in six figure jobs thinking that's the best they can do. My goal is to empower professionals to develop their own incremental Wealth & Riches® revenue rivers. Once you have identified your gifting and skill set, it is important that you begin to define and build your brand. People have to know you exist and that your services are for sale to benefit society.

I worked in marketing for over 25 years, spending over $1 billion for Fortune 500 and blue-chip advertisers. They invest heavily in their brand and keep a watchful eye on the competition. They launch new products and update old ones. The key is to constantly keep moving forward and never rest on your past success. Re-invention is critical for each of us. It becomes not about making money but about capitalizing on your true calling and building Wealth and Riches™ from your expertise. Jesus was an expert at providing salvation to the crowds that thronged him. He had the answer to their soul issue and they followed Him.

When Jesus launched his earthly ministry, he did not do it in a corner, he went to the religious Mecca at the time— Jerusalem. He was found at the big feasts. The audience was looking for him. They will look for you if you have defined your purpose, developed your expertise and made your true calling known to the world. Building your pot of oil into a self producing oil field will take time but it can be done a little at a time. Work on your talent and gift daily. Read. Study. Take Classes. Fifteen minutes a day working on your vision will build an empire.

Study the Wealth and Riches® Role Models –the lives of people who are doing what you desire to do. Follow their model and add your You-uniqueness®. Create your proprietary programs, camps, workshops, CDs, DVDs, books and begin to share your knowledge and insight with the world.

The world is thirsty for what God has placed inside of you. Dare to be creative. Spend time in solitude and develop a 90 Day plan.

My 90 Day Wealth and Riches Action Plan™

_____

_____

_____

_____

_____

_____

_____

_____

_____

_____

_____

_____

_____

8 BORROW NOT A FEW-DREAM IN BILLIONS™

Then he said, go, borrow thee vessels abroad, of all thy neighbours; even empty vessels; borrow not a few. 2 Kings 4:3

We set our own limitations. The widow was instructed to borrow empty vessels from all of her neighbors. Empty vessels have room for God to put His provision inside them. How much Wealth and Riches™ she would generate would be driven by her ability to sell her neighbors on the idea of giving her their empty vessels. Her instructions were to go abroad and ask of all her neighbors. It did not matter what type of vessel she collected as long as it was empty.

How many vessels did she collect?

The prophet told her to dream big…borrow not a few. I can see her going door to door and thinking, I have to collect lots of pots so the creditors will not take my sons. In the beginning, she had to work through her own fear and possible embarrassment at asking her neighbors.

Perhaps her neighbors felt sorry for her. Maybe they looked on her with pity or curiosity. She did not care. The reward would be the lives of her sons. She gained courage and her confidence began to grow. Her purpose overcame her fears. She had something noble to sell and that would generate the freedom of her sons. Her obedience opened up the windows of heaven.

We see the prophet's wife knocking on all her neighbor's doors and asking for empty vessels. She undoubtedly did not understand all that was happening inside her but she was obedient. When we are on the road to our destiny, we will not understand all the paths that God takes us, but we must keep moving and going to the next house of opportunity.

As we build our faith, the next knock becomes more faith filled. Her neighbors begin to give up their empty vessels. It was a small request; a vessel that was useless at the time was going to generate a huge return when mixed with faith. Some vessels were larger, some vessels were smaller. She kept collecting. I can almost hear her whispering under her breath, I will not be in this situation for long.

I believe she set a goal of collecting as many empty vessels as she could in the shortest amount of time. We often hear about how important it is to set goals. Why don't we set goals? I believe the complications of life or as the Bible calls it the cares of this world tend to block our ability to focus and concentrate on successful living.

The Lord told us in Habakkuk second chapter to write the vision and make it plain. A vision is seen in the supernatural realm. The ideas come to your head and thoughts, but we must listen to them.

Here are powerful statistics. Only three percent of adults have written goals that they work on every day. The other 97 percent have either vague and fuzzy goals or no goals at all.

The 3 percent who have clear, written specific goals earn five and ten times the amount of people without goals, even though they both start at the same starting line, with approximately the same abilities and opportunities, according to Brian Tracy.

What do you really want to do with your life?

_____

_____

_____

_____

_____

_____

It is important to renew your mind daily. How? Create

an altar in your home. Meet God there daily. Spend fifteen

minutes with God *first* in the morning. Spend fifteen

minutes with God before going to bed. Meditate Psalm 112

on the promises of living righteous. Create your own

Wealth and Riches Promise Diary™ with what you believe

God for. Put God first. Commit the first ten percent of

your increase for tithes before you pay your bills. Commit

to one to two percent for offerings and increase the

percentage until you get to twenty percent or more to tithes

and offerings as your income grows.

As you faith increases, take the Wealth and Riches

Action Steps™ to store your wealth for distribution. Open a

Dream Account e.g. a savings account. Start with five

percent of each pay cycle and increase to twenty percent. For example, start with five percent in March, eight percent in April, twelve percent in August, and twenty percent by December. Visualize the increase by meditating on the manifestation of money. Put a ten dollar bill in your purse and do not spend it. Each month increase it by ten dollars until you can carry a $100 bill in your purse that you do not spend.

Visualization brings crystallization. Spend thirty minutes a day (use your lunch hour to empower your dream) thinking about your dream. Create a Wealth and Riches Dream Bag™. Inside this bag, you will need a twelve month calendar to lay out your strategy for goal completion. You will also need a Wealth and Riches Daily Action Plan Journal™. In this journal you will record the steps you take each day to move you closer to your dream. Activity produces wealth. Another item you will need is the

Wealth and Riches Dreams and Goals Journal™ where you record your twelve month goals and your Wealth and Riches Vision Board™ for your life. Reading fuels the mind. Carry a book that excites you to execute your dream, most likely *Discover the Wealth that's in Your House* or *The Widow Oil Tycoon*. You will need a Bible, journal and pen.

Carry this Wealth and Riches Bag™ with you everywhere. You will be able to *steal* a few moments here and there to continuously renew your mind. Remember just fifteen minutes a day will build an empire.

Sign up for free daily emails of mentors and coaches e.g. National Organization of Women Business Owners has the Smart Brief or Wealth and Riches™ Today blog (Text MYDREAMLIFE to join our mailing list.) Be inspired by others. Visit Forbes online for women and other inspirational places. Grow your Vision.

See yourself prosperous. Feel the sensation of your

dream. Reduce your television time, unless it's a motivational program or a model of what you want to do in your business. Explore new things, new places, new stores, and new groups with like-minded people.

Attend Wealth and Riches Business Empowerment Conference™. Play songs that speak about increase over, over, over, and over again until you feel the breakthrough in your soul. One of my favorite songs is Viki Yohe's "Increase Me" with Alvin Slaughter.

If you can see it, you can achieve it. I enjoy my mobile office in Panera Bread. It has great food, a wonderful setting, free Wi-Fi and a great rewards program. Go shopping for your upcoming luxury items like a Cartier watch, Lexus car, Tory Burch bag, iPad—something way beyond your Present Financial Status® (PFS)

Visualize your ownership. Pray daily for God's wisdom. In thirty days, your entire world will begin to manifest change and increase!

Wealth and Riches Action Plan™

_____

_____

_____

_____

_____

_____

_____

_____

_____

_____

_____

_____

_____

This section is designed to help you re-focus your life and master goal setting. Now, take some time and write out your goals in the following nine categories. Write out what you would do if you have no limits. Remember with God we are limitless. Any limits you have placed on your life are self limits developed in childhood or throughout your life.

Each month work on a particular area and watch your life change. Be sure to write your goals down on a Wealth and Riches Manifestation Card™ and look at it throughout the day. Ask God for wisdom to bring it to pass. Develop a Wealth and Riches Action Plan™ to achieve success.

PERSONAL Goals & Wealth & Riches™ Action Steps

_____

_____

_____

_____

FAMILY Goals-Wealth & Riches™ Action Steps

_____

_____

_____

_____

FINANCIAL Goals-Wealth & Riches™ Action Steps

_____

_____

_____

CAREER Goals-Wealth & Riches™ Action Steps

_____

_____

_____

_____

BUSINESS Goals-Wealth & Riches™ Action Steps

_____

_____

_____

EDUCATION Goals-Wealth & Riches™ Action Steps

_____

_____

_____

HEALTH Goals-Wealth & Riches™ Action Steps

_____

_____

_____

_____

SOCIAL Goals-Wealth & Riches™ Action Steps

_____

_____

_____

_____

SPIRITUAL Goals-Wealth & Riches™ Action Steps

_____

_____

_____

Wealth and Riches™ Affirmation

There is that scattereth, and yet increaseth; and there is that

withholdeth more than is meet, but it tendeth to poverty. The liberal

soul shall be made fat; and he that watereth shall be watered also

himself. Proverbs 11:24-25.

9 SEE INCREASE EVERYWHERE

Now Jericho was straightly shut up because of the children of Israel: none went out, and none came in. And the LORD said unto Joshua, See, I have given into thine hand Jericho, and the king thereof, and the mighty men of valour. Joshua 6:1-2

We must train our spiritual eyes to see God's increase...everywhere even when facing a Jericho. A Jericho is an area of your life that seems impossible to overcome.

The city of Jericho was fortified. The walls were six feet thick and up to 26 feet high and sat on top of a 46 foot embankment. Its men of war were fearless and courageous warriors. Despite this natural picture, the Lord told Joshua to *see* I have a given you the city, the king and the mighty men of valour. Before the children of Israel took one step around the wall, God let Joshua know it was already done.

See your Jericho through God's eyes. Enlarge the vision of your life and the lives of your children. Do you see your Wealth and Riches Revenue Rivers™? These are rivers of ideas that He will give you that may seem insignificant or crazy at the time. If you move out and build a plan, the rivers will produce great Wealth and Riches® for you. Let's think in terms of *rivers* vs. streams.

Our God is huge. Write out what you see in your mind. Find pictures that resemble the dreams and visions that come to you. Writing your goals and visualizing them coming to pass really works.

This method works, trust me. My friends had been on a cruise and brought back an island picture frame covered with sea shells. I decided I wanted to go to the Caribbean and enjoy the powerful sun. I found a travel magazine and clipped out a picture of a lady in the Caribbean. She was standing on a white balcony that overlooked the ocean with its beautiful blue-green waters. I put the Caribbean picture on the frame and placed it on my desk.

Within ten days my husband and I received a phone call inviting us to go on a complimentary cruise to the Caribbean. Our cruise, airfare, and hotel were pre-paid by someone else. Wow.

In the book of Joshua and chapter six, the children of Israel were entering a new phase in their history. They watched as God opened up the Jordan river and they walked through on dry land. They witnessed miracle after miracle and now they faced a new obstacle—Jericho. In Joshua chapter five, the captain of the Lord's host appeared unto Joshua prior to this important challenge. God always touches us prior to major battles as we worship Him.

We are going to face challenges and tests or Jerichos that seem impossible to conquer on our way to Wealth and Riches™. The enemy wants to use our natural eye gate against us by causing us to focus on the natural aspect of vision. Naturally, the situation looked bleak. The city they were facing was straightly shut up because of the children of Israel. There was no access into the city by the physical eye.

Jesus often commented that they have eyes to see and cannot see (Mark 8:8). I did not understand that scripture during my earlier studies until I realized that we have both a natural and spiritual eye. The word of God says that we walk by faith and not by sight, but that is not easy to many of us. The enemy uses bills, letter from creditors, utility red letter disconnect notices, courtrooms, judges, district attorneys, lawsuits by banks (30-50 pages long) to try and intimidate us and threaten us. However, we must build up our faith by *speaking* and *believing* God's word. The more we speak and confess His word the more it becomes alive in our lives. The word of God must become greater than our physical word. Hebrews 11:1 says now faith is the substance of things hoped for and the evidence of things not seen.

Jericho is shut up. What financial situations in your life are currently straightly shut up? These situations seem impossible but things are not what they seem. Are the bill collectors threatening to shut off your utilities, seize your bank accounts, foreclose on your home, and ruin your credit reports? These are Wealth and Riches™ Jerichos. We know that nothing is too hard for God. Grab hold of His word and speak, confess and believe it. Ask God for the wisdom to bring your Jericho down. Authorize your financial angels to bring God's word to pass. Create an image of Wealth and Riches™ success (FFS-Future Financial Status™) that becomes greater than your PFS (Present Financial Situation™). There are many programs in your city to help with free legal advice. Ask God to direct your steps and get on the internet and search. Programs exist to cancel your mortgage debt---a form of financial forgiveness.

The Lord speaks to Joshua in the sixth chapter and encourages him to *see*. *See, I have given into thine hand Jericho, and the king thereof, and the mighty men of valor.* What a proclamation. When we open our spiritual eyes we see complete victory. The Lord speaks past tense, I have given into your hand. I love Him. It's already done.

We have to begin to train our spiritual eye to see. The things we see in the natural are temporal….just temporary. Put on your spiritual glasses and see that we already have the victory. We will take the city, the king and his might men. God gives Joshua a Wealth and Riches Action Plan™. Joshua and Israel had to participate in their solution. You are the solution to your problem. God has empowered you with the knowledge, power and resources to take your Jericho. We must do like Joshua and worship the Lord and ask what saith my Lord unto his servant. (Joshua 5:14).

God has the answers and will send people, programs into your life if you seek him day and night. Change your vision and see. See yourself walking in abundance. See your kids going to the best colleges on scholarships. See you sons and daughters becoming doctors. See yourself ministering all across the world. See yourself in your new home with its marble floors, circular driveway, luxury double bath, walk in closets the size of bedrooms and huge outdoor patio. See your new career and travelling over the world. See yourself speaking on stages across the world. See yourself on your radio and TV show. See yourself on the white sand beaches. See yourself building homes for orphans.

See yourself starting and building a multi-million dollar ministry or business empire. Dream Big. Visualize and design a Wealth and Riches Action Plan™ to bring it to pass. Faith without works is dead.

See increase in your Wealth and Riches™ every day. Release your mind. Unleash your increase. It's inside of you. Go! Go! Go! Take Wealth and Riches Action Steps™ that make your squeal with delight.

Do it even if you are afraid. Watch God open up every Jericho. It is *given into your hand*. Now you must take your promised land. Create a Wealth and Riches Dream Board™ of what you want to come to pass.

Wealth and Riches™ Action Plan

What do you see when you look at your Present Financial Status™ (PFS)? Are you walking in fear or faith?

_____

_____

_____

_____

_____

_____

Do you really believe God? Why or why not?

_____

_____

_____

_____

_____

_____

_____

What scriptures or promises of God do you believe for your restoration? What is your Jericho? Write your scripture promises here.

_____

_____

_____

_____

_____

_____

How often do you meditate and confess these scriptures? What Wealth and Riches Action Steps™ are you taking to bring the image that's in your mind to reality? Remember faith without works is dead.

Where are you financially? Not Enough, Just Enough, More Than Enough. Where are you mentally? What are your dominant thoughts? Are you focusing on God's word or thinking on your current financial situation?

Wealth and Riches™ Action Plan

If you want to change your outcome, you will need to change your thinking. Visualize your Jericho as already defeated. What does your life look like if your Jericho is gone?

If you are experiencing lack, then you are thinking lack. Meditate daily on Psalm 112. Confess multiple times throughout the day, Wealth and Riches™ are in my house. It is important to engage you entire family. In the next seven days, I am going to implement the following changes in my life.

_____

_____

_____

_____

_____

10 GO, SELL, PAY OFF DEBTS & LIVE

And it came to pass, when the vessels were full that she said unto her son, Bring me yet a vessel. And he said unto her, There is not a vessel more. And the oil stayed. Then she came and told the man of God. And he said, Go sell the oil, and pay thy debt, and live thou and thy children of the rest. 2 Kings 4:6-7

God is working behind the scenes of time to give back the Wealth and Riches™ to Christians who suffered loss during this economic season. I want to encourage you to believe in God to restore whatever you may have lost and begin to take the Wealth and Riches™ building steps to restore your faith in Him.

In second book of Kings chapter eight, we are introduced to a woman whose son had been restored to life. She had a prophet who knew the heart of God and could foretell the economic future. He warned her that a famine was coming. She listened to the man of God.

If we are connected to God, the Lord will warn His people in advance that tough times are ahead and to brace ourselves. When I worked in corporate America, I was led to move my 401K funds into government securities just a few months before the stock market crashed and lost trillions of dollars in value.

The Lord had called for a famine upon the land and it was going to last seven years. The woman listened and believed the man of God and took preventive action to escape the hardship. She escaped by moving to the land of the Philistines for seven years.

After the seven years were up, she went to cry unto the king for her house and her land. She owned possessions that were lost during the famine, but she had incredible faith in God to believe that He would restore anything that she may have lost. She had remarkable confidence. She had an expectation of restoration.

She not only believed, but took the Wealth and Riches Action Steps™ to recover her property. We as Christians have the same expectation that whatever was lost during the economic downturn will be restored to us again. The Lord has not forgotten anything we lost.

In Joel 2:25 we have a promise that he will restore to you the *years* that the locust hath eaten, the cankerworm, and the caterpillar, and the palmerworm. I have held onto this promise for years. This word is being manifested in my life even as I finalize this chapter.

Wealth and Riches™ Restoration Assessment

What wealth have you lost during the great recession?

_____

_____

_____

Do you believe that the Lord will restore your losses? Why or why not?

_____

_____

_____

What Wealth and Riches Action Steps™ are you taking to regain wealth? _____

_____

_____

To regain your restoration, we must operate as the woman in second Kings. When the famine was over, she went to the king with to cry for her house and land. Have you cried to God for your Wealth and Riches™?

We see that the Lord was working on her side at the same time. The King was talking to Gehazi, the prophet's servant about the woman's testimony when she *just happened* to walk in to see the king. Some call it fate. Others call it a coincidence. As believers, we know it was a divine appointment.

The Lord was already working behind the scenes. Her faith led her to the king at the exact time he was hearing about her from Gehazi.

God has you on the hearts and minds of those who will restore your Wealth and Riches™. You may get some crazy ideas to go places and meet people, but do not be afraid as God opens doors.

Divine set ups occur in strange places. As a result of her faith and Wealth and Riches Action Steps™, this lady received all that was hers and received interest. The king appointed for her a certain officer and instructed the officer to restore *all* that was hers, and all the fruits of the field since the day that she left the land, even until now.

Seven years of your Wealth and Riches™ that has been held up is being released. Nothing will be lost. God held her increase in *escrow* for her. There are some things that He has held for us and will pay us interest.

We have to develop the same faith and expectation that the Lord is going to restore unto us all that was lost during the last seven years. In other words, if we walk with the Lord with expectation, we do not lose because He pays back everything we would have earned.

Wealth and Riches Action Plan™

What was your income in your highest earning season?

_____

_____

What is your income now?

Do you believe it can be restored and increased? Why or why not?

_____

_____

_____

Use the power of the Word to increase your faith. Pull your credit report to see what you need to work on to regain your wealth. Begin today to make the daily changes that will change your future. Little by little, day by day. Keep moving forward.

Our widow heroine in second Kings the fourth chapter knew how to be obedient. The prophet told her to go, borrow empty vessels from of all her neighbors and to borrow not a few. We have to develop an outlook of Wealth and Riches™ by gathering containers or jars to put the oil or provision that the Lord is going to pour into our vessels. The Lord will only provide according to our ability to gather.

One of our biggest jars is our ability to produce *ideas* that bring in Wealth and Riches™. We set our own limitations. The widow was instructed to borrow vessels from her neighbors that were empty (or had room to put God's provision in) and to *borrow not a few*. How much Wealth and Riches™ she would generate would be driven by her ability and talent to persuade her neighbors to give up their empty vessels and by her ability to collect as many as she could see.

How many jars can you fit in your house? Would you have collected ten or twenty or millions of empty vessels? The limit is set by the vision you have for your life.

The widow's business was a family business. She understood the power of many. She and her sons shut up in her house and began to pour out into all those vessels and set aside that which is full. We must shut out the voices or the negative spectators in our lives. In the Bible story, we see her sons working to bring the vessels to her and she did the pouring. She poured according to her faith. Faith is personal. Faith ignores the words of the dream killers. The results for your life are totally up to you. Faith ignores the words of the dream killers. The widow kept telling her sons to bring her a vessel. She was letting them know that Jesus provides, but we have to participate in the provision. Bring me some more empty jars, she said.

The oil did not cease until all the empty vessels were full and there was no more vessels to hold the Wealth and Riches™ in. She determined how much wealth she was going to produce. When the vessels ran out, the oil stayed. The word stay is also used in our financial systems today. When you have a stay from your creditors, they cannot touch you unless the judge says so. God is our judge and

He will protect his people. We must not cast away our confidence in Him.

Finally she went back to the man of God and he shared with her the final secret. He did not give her the entire solution until she was obedient to the first thing he told her...go and borrow vessels and not a few. God opens doors according to our obedience. What has He told you to do that you have not done yet? Do that and then come back to Him for next steps.

Nothing in the house but a jar of oil yielded a huge increase when added to faith and obedience. The final command from the man of God was simple: to *go, sell the oil, pay off thy debt and live you and your children on the rest.*

It's the same message God is saying to us today. We must "go," sell our oil, pay off our debts and live on the rest...we and our children. He is the God of abundance.

ABOUT THE AUTHOR

L. Renee Richardson is the Founder and CEO of Women of Vision and Destiny Ministries, Wealth & Riches Today Inc. and the Rich Gurlz Club. The global headquarters is in Chicago, Illinois with offices in Columbus, Georgia, Phenix City Ala, and Fort Benning region.

L. Renee graduated magna cum laude from Columbus State University (BBA) and the University of Georgia (MBA).

She has a unique teaching gift and talent to empower individuals and organizations to tap into their hidden wealth. She believes that everyone has untapped revenue in their homes, businesses, careers and ministries.

Her success in the corporate, business, and ministry worlds makes her insights and wisdom powerful and life changing. She has spent $1 billion in advertising for Fortune 500 companies for over 25 years and is known as the *Billionaire Visionnaire.*™ L. Renee has worked in ministry for 35 years for small and mega churches. She began preaching at age 13, teaching Sunday School at age 16 and wrote Christian stage plays in her youth.

L. Renee is committed to what she has passionately advised others to do all her life: Live Your Rich BIG Dreams...Today! ™ L. Renee's mission is to empower aspiring entrepreneurs, corporate executives and ministry leaders to hit a million in revenue. It all starts with a written vision and business action plan to design a legacy that endures and lasts for generations.

Wealth and Riches Today Inc. spearheads this message through its full service business boutique specializing in business structure, incorporation, branding, marketing, public relations, publishing, conferences, business coaching, and business spa retreats at exclusive resorts.

In 2000, L. Renee birthed Women of Vision and Destiny, Inc. (WOVD), an international women's leadership center which will celebrate 19 years of global service. WOVD has empowered over 550,000 women and young ladies to make an impact on their world. We have an chapter in India.

While travelling over 400,000 miles in corporate America, L. Renee and her husband Glen opened a Marble Slab Creamery franchise, a premium ice cream shop in August 2007 on Michigan Avenue. The business earned $1 million in sales, served over 1.2 million multi-cultural guests, and hired over 100 youth, mostly urban teens. After the business closed, L. Renee gained a new revelation of Wealth and Riches™ and has a huge heart for those who are going through the darkest seasons of their life.

Distinguished as one of Chicago's Most Powerful Business Women and one of the Marketing industry's most Powerful Execs, L. Renee has received esteemed recognition for her expertise within the *Chicago Tribune, Chicago Sun Times, Media Post, Fox 32, WGN and Ad week magazines;* and has been featured in *Jet Magazine, Black Enterprise, Precious Times, and Grace Today* magazines, for her trailblazing career accomplishments. Renee was honored by *Grace Today* magazine with its Women in Business Award. She has also been featured on Black Enterprise TV in her corner office in downtown Chicago.

L. Renee speaks nationally and internationally. She served on panel for entrepreneurs for the Women's Business Development Center in Chicago. She was a speaker at *Black Enterprise's* first Women of Power Summit.

Let's Stay Connected

L. Renee Richardson can be reached for speaking

engagements at Lrenee@wealthandrichestoday.com

Text **MYDREAMLIFE** to join our mailing list.

Visit www.wealthandrichestoday..com

Follow her on Twitter at @todaywealth

Follow her on Instagram @lreneerichsrdson

Join *L. Renee Richardson on Facebook* at:

L. Renee Richardson (Public Figure)

Women of Vision and Destiny Ministries, Inc.

Wealth & Riches Today, Inc.

Rich Gurlz Club

Monet Studios

World Headquarters-Chicago

Offices: Columbus, GA/Phenix City, AL/ Fort Benning

Phone: 312-493-4770

Join us Monday-Friday 6 a.m. Power UP Your Faith Show

Dial In 712-770-4615 Access Code: 681626

International Numbers Available.